SPORTS
ALL-STARS

SIMONE
BILES

2ND EDITION

Jon M. Fishman

Lerner Publications ◆ Minneapolis

Lerner Publications Company
An imprint of Lerner Publishing Group, Inc.
241 First Avenue North
Minneapolis, MN 55401 USA

For reading levels and more information, look up this title at www.lernerbooks.com.

Main body text set in Albany Std. Typeface provided by Agfa.

Editor: Brianna Kaiser **Photo Editor:** Brianna Kaiser

Library of Congress Cataloging-in-Publication Data

Names: Fishman, Jon M., author.
Title: Simone Biles / Jon M. Fishman.
Description: 2nd edition. | Minneapolis: Lerner Publications, 2021. | Series: Sports all-stars | Includes bibliographical references and index. | Audience: Ages 7–11 | Audience: Grades 2–3 | Summary: "Since storming the 2016 Olympics, gymnast Simone Biles keeps pushing the boundaries of her sport. Learn about Biles's gravity-defying moves, what she does outside gymnastics, and why her fans love to see her compete"— Provided by publisher.
Identifiers: LCCN 2020036295 (print) | LCCN 2020036296 (ebook) | ISBN 9781728404387 (library binding) | ISBN 9781728423166 (paperback) | ISBN 9781728418841 (ebook)
Subjects: LCSH: Biles, Simone, 1997– —Juvenile literature. | Gymnasts—United States—Biography—Juvenile literature. | Women gymnasts—United States—Biography—Juvenile literature.
Classification: LCC GV460.2.B55 F57 2021 (print) | LCC GV460.2.B55 (ebook) | DDC 796.44092 [B]—dc23

LC record available at https://lccn.loc.gov/2020036295
LC ebook record available at https://lccn.loc.gov/2020036296

Manufactured in the United States of America
1-48496-49010-9/30/2020

TABLE OF CONTENTS

GOLD
GETTER

Simone Biles on the balance beam during the 2019 world championships

Simone Biles had a record-setting performance at the 2019 USA Gymnastics National Championships in Kansas City, Missouri. She won the vault, balance beam, and floor exercise events. She also won her sixth all-around national title.

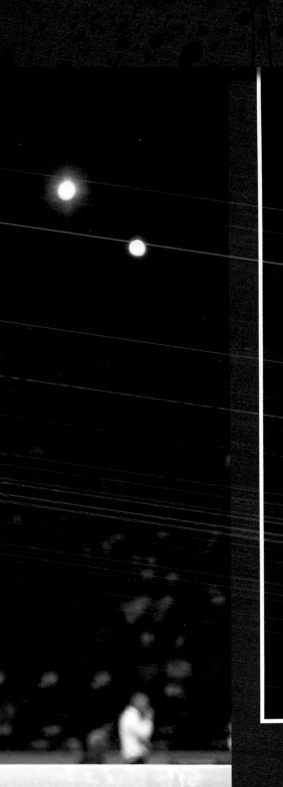

FACTS
AT A GLANCE

- **Date of Birth:** March 14, 1997

- **Position:** gymnast

- **League:** USA Gymnastics

- **Professional Highlights:** won her 25th world medal in 2019 to set the record for most championship medals by any gymnast; won her fifth world championship all-around title in 2019; helped Team USA win all-around gold at the 2016 Olympic Games

- **Personal Highlights:** had one of her floor moves, the Biles, added to the official gymnastics rule book in 2013; placed fourth on *Dancing with the Stars* in 2017; cowrote *Courage to Soar: A Body in Motion, a Life in Balance* in 2016

Biles flips during her floor exercise at the 2019 world championships.

At nationals, Biles became the first woman to land two new moves in competition. First, she performed the triple-twisting double somersault in the floor exercise competition. She twisted three times in the air while doing two backflips. Then she did the double-twisting double somersault dismount on the balance beam. Biles flipped backward off the beam and twisted twice in the air while doing two backward somersaults—both incredibly difficult and dangerous moves. The International Gymnastics Federation discourages other gymnasts from performing them because of the risk of serious injury if they fail to land the moves.

   With the US national championships behind her, Biles was ready to take on the 2019 world championships in Stuttgart, Germany. She began the competition on October 8 by helping Team USA win all-around gold for the fifth year in a row. Then she turned her focus to the individual all-around title. Although she placed fifth in the uneven bars event, she won gold medals for vault, balance beam, and floor exercise. She won the women's all-around title. Her impressive performance made her the first woman to win five all-around world titles. It was also her 25th world medal, setting a new record for most medals by any gymnast!

LEARNING TO SOAR

Biles performs a floor routine in 2013.

Simone Biles was born on March 14, 1997, in Columbus, Ohio. She grew up in Spring, Texas, with her younger sister, Adria, after the girls were adopted by their grandparents. Both sisters loved to jump and tumble.

Simone taught herself to flip backward off a mailbox. One day, her day care group went on a field trip to a gym. Simone saw gymnasts practicing their routines. The young girl copied them by trying her own moves.

Simone's adoptive parents, Ron and Nellie, received a letter a short time later. It was from

Biles's parents, Ron and Nellie, watch her perform at the 2019 world championships.

the gym. One of the coaches had noticed Simone flipping and rolling. The coach suggested Simone start practicing at the gym. Ron and Nellie agreed that gymnastics would be a great fit for their daughter.

About one year later, Simone began working with Aimee Boorman. The coach believed in Simone's talent and thought she could be great in the gym. But Boorman had never worked with a top-level gymnast before. "We were kind of both clueless about it," Simone said. "So we were just learning together."

Aimee Boorman with Biles before a competition in 2016. Boorman began coaching Biles in 2003.

Simone learned fast. By the age of 10, she was competing against top gymnasts her age from around the country. She was at the junior elite level four years later. Two years after that, Simone burst onto the international gymnastics scene in a big way. She had the top scores at the 2013 world championships to take the all-around title. Her floor exercise really wowed the crowd. "On floor, I just have a lot of fun," Simone said. "That is the main key."

Being named 2013 world champion was just the beginning for Simone. She won the title again in 2014. Then, in 2015, she won the all-around world championship for the third year in a row. She became the first woman to win the world title three straight times. In 2016, she would get her chance to add Olympic medals to her trophy case.

Biles stays focused
during training.

In 2019, Biles performs the triple-twisting double somersault during the floor exercise competition at the world championships.

Simone Biles has ruled the highest level of gymnastics since 2013. She's a world champion and an Olympic champion. She even has four gymnastics moves named after her. She's brimming with athletic talent. But to stay on top, talent isn't enough. She works *really* hard.

In 2013, Biles's lower leg was sore after she landed a certain way. She and Coach Boorman came up with a new way to land. The new way felt better, but it wasn't easy. The new move became known as the Biles, and it's in the official gymnastics rule book.

Biles spends 32 hours each week training in the gym. She spreads that time over six days. Stretching her muscles is a big part of her daily workout. Stretching helps prevent injury. It also allows Biles's arms and legs to reach the extreme positions her routines call for. She stretches on her own and with coaches and teammates.

Part of Biles's time in the gym is spent practicing basic skills. These include the flips and spins that make up her routines. To make a skill perfect, Biles does it over and over and over again. When it comes time to perform in a meet, she barely has to think about the skill to do it just right.

Cardio training is another part of Biles's

Biles warms up with her teammates.

workouts. The star athlete doesn't want to get tired during a meet. In the gym, Biles will practice a skill such as backflips. Then she'll run back to where she started and do it again without pausing. Cardio training makes her heart and lungs strong.

Biles stretches with teammate
Jordan Chiles during practice in 2019.

To get ready for a meet, Biles puts her skills together to create a routine. She links her flips and twists with leaps and turns. She practices to make sure everything works together. At the meet, Biles will be judged in part by how smoothly her routine flows.

Biles mostly eats healthful food. The gymnast knows that if she doesn't eat well, she won't perform well. That means lots of egg whites, fish, and chicken. Before a workout, she eats bananas with peanut butter. Biles says the snack helps prevent muscle cramps.

Sometimes Biles eats less nutritious snacks. She likes soda. And after a big meet, it's time to celebrate! "It doesn't even matter if I don't win," she says. "After every meet I have pizza. Pepperoni pizza."

Biles works on her skills by doing flips.

OFF THE
MAT

Biles leads the Houston Texans onto the field before a 2019 NFL football game.

Biles's friends and family don't think of her as a superstar athlete.

At her parents' home, she laughs with her parents and argues with her sister. She also plays with the family's four German

Biles began to go to school at home at the age of 13. Learning at home helped her keep up with her gym schedule. But she didn't like it. She missed seeing her friends every day.

shepherds: Maggie, Atlas, Bella, and Lily. She loves to shop and get her nails done.

Biles says her favorite food is Italian, and she loves to eat at Olive Garden. She likes the TV show *Pretty Little Liars* and the Hunger Games books. She dances to popular new songs. When she's with her friends, Biles feels like an ordinary young person.

To the rest of the world, Biles is a star on and off the mat. She appeared on the cover of *Sports Illustrated* and other magazines. She has been on TV shows such as *Fox & Friends*, *The Ellen DeGeneres Show*, and *Today*.

In 2016, Biles talks about her book, Courage to Soar, in New York.

Biles didn't slow down after the 2016 Olympics. She cowrote a book about her life, *Courage to Soar: A Body in Motion, a Life in Balance*. In 2017, she placed fourth on the TV show *Dancing with the Stars*. She also moved into her own home and got two dogs, Lilo and Rambo.

female gymnast. Being short can help athletes perform better spins and flips. In 2016, it helped Biles become an Olympic champion. The smallest member of Team USA carried the flag for her country at the closing ceremony in Rio de Janeiro.

Biles carries the US flag during the Olympics closing ceremony.

"THE FIRST SIMONE BILES"

Biles gives a gold-medal performance with her floor routine.

The 2016 Olympics was a huge success for the United States and Biles. They won gold in the team event, and Biles became the Olympic all-around champion!

Biles (*center*) stands with Aliya Mustafina (*left*) and Aly Raisman (*right*) during a medal ceremony. Biles won one bronze and four gold medals at the Rio Olympics.

She won five Olympic medals. That made it one of the most successful Olympics ever for a US athlete. Fans compared her to some of the greatest Olympians of all time. "I'm not a celebrity," she said. "I'm not the next Usain Bolt or Michael Phelps. I'm the first Simone Biles."

Biles and her teammates joined the Kellogg's Tour of Gymnastics Champions after the Olympics. The tour visited 36 cities in the United States, bringing world-

Biles flips on the beam at the 2019 US national championships.

class gymnastics to the fans. Once the tour was over, she took a break from gymnastics. In January 2018, she revealed that she had been abused by USA Gymnastics team doctor Larry Nassar. "It was a weight that I carried so heavily on my chest, so I felt like, if I shared it with people, then it would be a relief for me," Biles said. Nassar abused many young women under his care. In 2018, he was sentenced to life in prison.

Biles returned to gymnastics in July 2018 at the US Classic. She won the all-around title! She went on to place first in every event at the US national championships and to win all-around at the world championships. Her winning streak continued in 2019. She won the all-around competition at the Stuttgart World Cup, the GK US Classic, the US national championships, and the world championships.

Biles performs on the uneven bars in 2019.

With her talent, it's no wonder Biles was chosen to represent the US in the 2020 Summer Olympics in Tokyo, Japan. But then COVID-19 swept the world. The dangerous disease was making millions of people sick. Gyms closed, and the Summer Olympics was postponed until 2021 or later. But Biles kept training. "Going in every day knowing and hoping 2021 is on the horizon keeps me going," she said.

Biles practices her balance beam routine in 2019.

Biles talks to her coaches Cecile (*left*) and Laurent Landi (*middle*) during practice in 2019.

Since she couldn't go to the gym, Biles worked out at home. She ran sprints at a local track and walked her dogs. She also did online video sessions with her coaches, Cecile and Laurent Landi, three days a week. By mid-May, her gym reopened and she resumed training in person. As she keeps working hard and building her skills, Biles will no doubt continue to have success both on and off the mat.

All-Around Gold-Medal Winners

2016 Simone Biles, United States
2012 Gabby Douglas, United States
2008 Nastia Liukin, United States
2004 Carly Patterson, United States
2000 Simona Amânar, Romania
1996 Lilia Podkopayeva, Ukraine

Team Final Gold-Medal-Winning Country

2016 United States
2012 United States
2008 China
2004 Romania
2000 Romania
1996 United States

Glossary

all-around: a competition in which female gymnasts compete alone on vault, uneven bars, balance beam, and floor exercise

balance beam: a narrow beam on which gymnasts perform. This is also the name of an event in gymnastics.

cardio: a type of workout designed to get the heart pumping and improve blood flow

dismount: to get down from something, such as a balance beam

elite: the top level of gymnastics

floor exercise: an event in which gymnasts perform dance steps and tumbling moves to music on a 40-square-foot (3 sq. m) mat

meet: a large competition with many gymnastics events

routine: a combination of skills

team final: a competition in which female gymnasts compete as a team on vault, uneven bars, balance beam, and floor exercise

uneven bars: an event in which gymnasts perform on two bars, one high and one low

vault: an event in which gymnasts launch from a springboard to a vaulting table and then into the air

Source Notes

10 Julia Fincher, "Who Is . . . Simone Biles," NBCOlympics.com, July 29, 2016, http://archiverio.nbcolympics.com/news/who -simone-biles.

11 Associated Press, "Simone Biles Crowned Gymnastics All-Around World Champion," Team USA, October 4, 2013, http:// www.teamusa.org/News/2013/October/04/Simone-Biles -Crowned-Gymnastics-All-Around-World-Champion.

17 Caroline Praderio, "Here's What Simone Biles Eats before and after She Competes," *Business Insider*, August 12, 2016, http://mobile.businessinsider.com/simone-biles-diet-2016-8.

23 James Masters, "Simone Biles Wins All-Around Gold at Rio Games in US One-Two," *CNN*, last modified August 12, 2016, http://edition.cnn.com/2016/08/11/sport/simone-biles-usa -gymnastics-rio.

24 Abby Aguirre, "Simone Biles on Overcoming Abuse, the Postponed Olympics, and Training during a Pandemic," *Vogue*, July 9, 2020, https://www.vogue.com/article/simone -biles-cover-august-2020.

26 Ben Kesslen, "Simone Biles Says of Uncertainty around Tokyo Olympics, 'We Train as If,'" *NBC*, July 23, 2020, https:// www.nbcnews.com/news/sports/simone-biles-says -uncertainty-around-tokyo-olympics-we-train-if-n1234676.

Nicks, Erin. *Best Female Gymnasts of All Time*. Minneapolis: Abdo, 2020.

Olympics
https://www.olympic.org

Scarbrough, Mary. *Simone Biles*. Vero Beach, FL: Rourke Educational Media, 2020.

Scheff, Matt. *The Summer Olympics: World's Best Athletic Competition*. Minneapolis: Lerner Publications, 2021.

Simone Biles
https://www.simonebiles.com

Team USA: Simone Biles
https://www.teamusa.org/usa-gymnastics/athletes/simone -biles

Index

Photo Acknowledgments

Image credits: AP Photo/Amy Sanderson, pp. 4-5, 9, 26; AP Photo/Kunihiko Miura, p. 6; AP Photo/Charles Krupa, p. 8; AP Photo/Tony Gutierrez, p. 10; A.Ricardo/ Shutterstock.com, pp. 12, 17; AP Photo/Kydpl Kyodo, p. 13; AP Photo/Gregory Bull, p. 15; AP Photo/Charlie Riedel, pp. 16, 24; AP Photo/Eric Christian Smith, p. 18; Steve Mack/Alamy Stock Photo, p. 20; AP Photo/Matt Dunham, p. 21; Petr Toman/ Shutterstock.com, p. 22; Leonard Zhukovsky/Shutterstock.com, p. 23; AP Photo/ Marijan Murat, p. 25; AP Photo/Melissa J. Perenson, p. 27.

Cover: The Asahi Shimbun/Getty Images.